STORMS
in the Northland

A Gothic Tale of Youth
Glensheen Mansion, Marjorie Congdon,
and
Two Old Lady's Adventures

by BJ Burke

STORMS in the Northland

Copyright © 2020 BJ Burke

Photographs and artwork used with permission of *Star Tribune* and *Pioneer Press*.

Cover photo: *Surf's Up on Lake Superior.* Used with permission from Dennis O'Hara of Northern Images Studio.

Editing and design by Jansina of Rivershore Books

Library of Congress Control Number: 2023915396

ISBN: 978-1-63522-127-5

Printed in the United States of America
10 9 8 7 6 5 4 3 2 1

Rivershore Books
8982 Van Buren St. NE • Minneapolis, MN 55434
612-208-3434 • info@rivershorebooks.com

To my Husband

*My knight on a
white horse!*

Acknowledgements

Many thanks for encouragement and interest in my stories to:

June Anderson for her hours spent reading, editing, and suggestions.

Mac MacKechnie for the time he spent rewriting and believing in this unique twist on a well-known Minnesota story.

Writing agent, John Lehman, for the encouragement he gave to the new writer of a gothic, twisted story of youth and evil.

Mille Lacs Messenger
Alycia Van Rheenen

Mille Lacs Energy Cooperative/Crow Wing County

Special Granddaughter for use of her wedding photos.

Sincere thanks to Mary Henderson for her gift of poetry.

Thanks to Karlajo McKean for artwork memorial of Gordon McKean; a drawing of the most popular lighthouse in Minnesota.

Preface

One day in the 1990s, I was sitting in my car after touring the stately, well-publicized estate of Chester and Clara Congdon. Better known as the Glensheen Mansion, it is located just north of Duluth, Minnesota, on the North Shore of Lake Superior. The property is now owned by the University of Minnesota, which had just started to promote the architecture and luxury of the home and conduct tours of the estate. It is open daily for the public to view, and thousands of tourists tour it yearly.

Tears welled up in my eyes as I remembered the joy I had felt when one of the Congdon daughters gave me my first wedding shower. I was the luckiest, proudest young woman around to receive such attention from this well-known, wealthy woman in my church. This story will tell you of how naïve I was at age nineteen, convinced that dear, sweet Marjorie Congdon LeRoy could do no wrong.

Will to Murder, a book published in 1998 by Gail Feichtinger, tells of six-year-old Marjorie, who was adopted by Elisabeth Congdon, the unmarried daughter of Chester and Clara Congdon. A quiet, bookish child, Marjorie was a loner who was often in trouble. She stole things from local stores, and her mother covered up her bad behavior rather than blemish the good name of the Congdons. Stories abound about Marjorie's obsessions for wanting things, then quickly tiring of them, but most of all they tell of her obsession with money and setting fires.

Contents

Part 1

Of Innocence and Evil

I was sixteen years old in 1958 and a member of the United Methodist Church. My mother was active in the church, helping in the women's circle by serving food to members and for funerals and special events. I sang in the choir, enjoyed the youth group, and most of all I adored managing the young "Children's Crying Room" during church services. The church and its minister were an important part of my life.

I came from a working-class family. My grandparents, maternal and paternal, had eight living children. My father worked on the railroad and was rarely at home; my mother, a committed homemaker, was in charge of the family—my brother and me.

I had enjoyed babysitting since age 13 and, unless I was sick, I never missed a Sunday caring for the little ones in the crying room. I felt it was a big contribution to the church and it allowed the children's parents to attend church services. On any given Sunday I might find myself caring for several tiny babies in cribs and three toddlers on the floor.

From 1958 to 1960 I took care of two special little children. These toddlers were dropped off at the door, always wearing white shirts, black ties, and navy-blue double-breasted navy type jackets. They were well-behaved, cute, and very good with the other children. Groomed beyond perfection, they could have just stepped out of a children's modeling magazine.

I was told by Church Board members "in the know" that their mother was Marjorie Congdon LeRoy, wife of Richard LeRoy, a man who was head of a prominent insurance company and running for the State Legislature as well. Mr. and Mrs. LeRoy had four children, close in age. The children's mother, Marjorie, was on the church board and well-known in Minnesota. I was impressed with the family but unaware of the prominence of the Congdon family name in Duluth. I only knew I adored these beautiful, well-behaved little children who were so fun and friendly.

Because of the children, I also paid attention to their mom. Small in stature and weight and finely groomed, she wore very thick glasses, specially tailored clothing, and an amber-eyed fox fur collar. Her skin was smooth and beautiful; her shiny brown hair was always pulled up smoothly on top of her head with nary a hair out of place. She was pristine and prestigious in appearance and the beauty of the children complemented her good looks. The family was full of energy, intelligent, and independent. I liked Mrs. LeRoy because she always went out of her way to tell me what a great job I did with her children and how much she appreciated it—to say nothing of the fact that my teenage self was in awe of her beauty and standing in the church.

In June 1960 I announced I was engaged and planning to be married in the church the following June. I wanted our minister to perform the ceremony. I had graduated from high school and was working full time. My future husband, Jack, and I had been dating for two years, were best friends, and were comfortable in each other's arms. I was amazed—actually dumbfounded—when Marjorie LeRoy asked me if she could give my first wedding shower in her home. She said it was for all of the good things I had done for her children and the church. Had I heard her right? I said, "You don't have to do that, Mrs. LeRoy; I enjoy working for our church."

She replied, "But I really love parties and want to do this for you. It will be so much fun!"

When I confided to my mom that I wasn't sure if this was right, she said, "It is a wonderful gift; why not?" She could not have known how much I idolized Marjorie LeRoy. Mrs. LeRoy told me to give her a list of family, friends, and attendants and she would do all of the rest. I knew that in addition to having a large personality, she was extremely efficient. She took control and began making her plans for my one-of-a-kind bridal shower.

The Bridal Shower

On the day of my bridal shower, I nervously walked into her home in South Minneapolis. It was elegant with a huge stairway leading to the second floor, glowing wood floors, shining tile, and antique furniture. Not an item was out of place, and everything was polished to the nines. I could not believe Mrs. LeRoy would go to such work and expense for me. I was so impressed, as were my family and friends who, like me, all lived modest lives in modest homes. Marjorie was the supreme hostess, laughing and visiting with everyone, talking about the plans for the wedding, my dress, and the wonderful minister who would be marrying us.

Approximately sixteen family and friends attended my gala event. Marjorie had decorated the luncheon table with white lace runners down the center of the long dining room table. A huge cut glass crystal bowl in the middle was overflowing with green grapes covered in shimmering glazed sugar.

(How *did* Mrs. LeRoy know I loved lace and cut crystal?) She served chicken salad, fresh watermelon cut in perfectly round balls topped with sweet syrup, and buttery croissants so each guest could make their sandwich with fresh cheeses and assorted meats. Desserts were an assortment of small tarts and treats. What a buffet! The likes of it I had never seen before!

GEORGIAN SILVER GRACES THE HEPPLEWHITE MAHOGANY-AND-SATINWOOD SIDEBOARD
MRS. RICHARD LE ROY'S DINING ROOM
'The real fun is the hunting and the saving up for something you want'

Marjorie suggested we open gifts. There were many items for Jack and me to use in our future home: lots of kitchen items, dishes, and pots and pans. I told everyone how I appreciated every one of them and thanked Mrs. LeRoy for hosting this exciting shower. She said, "I enjoyed every minute of it!" Then, handing me an elegant foil gold box, she said, "I have purchased one more special gift—something special for your honeymoon."

When I opened the present, I was shocked to see an elegant and expensive white lace and silk peignoir set, a nightgown and lace robe to match with tiny pearls sewn in the neck and sleeves. I was overcome with emotion. Such luxury I had never experienced before. I felt rich, indulged, and all of the other emotions that wealth allows. To say I was impressed with such sharing, such luxury, from a woman who did not know me well, would be an understatement. I was overwhelmed.

In June of 1961, I started my life as a married woman. I had a loving new husband, wonderful friends, both old and new, a new apartment, and a good job. Life was great! I saw Marjorie LeRoy only a couple of times after the wedding as we moved away and found a church home closer to our new home, but Marjorie was still a very special person in my life. I prized the peignoir nightgown set she had given me for our honeymoon and for many years thereafter wore it for our anniversaries.

In 1963 our first son, Adam, was born. It was a difficult Cesarean-section birth in a day when that rarely occurred. Adam weighed in at ten pounds. I spent thirteen days in the hospital, but I felt God had repaid me for every minute of my volunteering for the church.

One day I received a small box in the mail addressed to: "Master Adam Clough." When I opened the box, wrapped in baby blue tissue paper was a tiny sterling silver baby rattle with Adam's name monogrammed on it. The note said, "Thinking of you today. From Marjorie LeRoy," the special lady who had shown me a bit of luxury when I was a new bride.

Glensheen Mansion

Over the years I became aware of Chester and Claire Congdon's contributions to the City of Duluth. I began connecting the history and stories I had heard and the articles I had read about Glensheen Mansion. The most expensive house in Duluth, Glensheen was built in 1908 by Chester Congdon, son of a Methodist minister. Chester was a lawyer, US Assistant Attorney, a builder, and an Iron Range ore magnate, part of the rich US Steel Corporation.

Glensheen was designed by Clarence Johnston, the same man who designed the Northrup Auditorium and Anoka State Hospital. At the time, Glensheen was said to have cost $854,000, the equivalent of $22 million in today's market.

A large portion of that cost was for the interior furnishings of this huge house. Glensheen sits directly on Lake Superior on more than 20 acres of beautiful natural woods, spruce trees and birches with a creek running through to the lake. The Jacobean style architecture is of majestic beauty, and the interior thirty-nine rooms with carved oak wall panels and staircases speak to a luxurious lifestyle. There are shiny marble floors and imported ceramic tiles. Many items were imported from foreign countries.

Claire and Chester Congdon had six living children. One of the daughters, Elisabeth, never married and lived with her mother after her father's sudden death. She was active in all manner of nursing as were her mother and grandmother. She had survived breast cancer, stroke, and diabetes only to be murdered in bed at age 83, smothered by a pink satin pillow. Her private nurse, Velma Pietila, was bludgeoned to death with a brass candleholder at the same time.

Elisabeth had adopted two daughters, Marjorie and Jennifer. As I learned more about the Congdons, the lights were going off in my brain. The woman I admired and felt such gratitude for, Marjorie Congdon LeRoy, was one of Elisabeth's adopted daughters.

Maturing Years

Over the next six years, Jack and I had three babies, two boys and a girl, and we grew into a bigger, newer home. Life kept me very busy. One Sunday I attended a service at my parents' church, where I learned that Mrs. LeRoy had been divorced at Richard LeRoy's request. I felt angry, believing he had only married Marjorie for her name and money to help him get into the Minnesota State Legislature. All those beautiful children and then he left. It bothered me! I was told his former wife had moved out of state with her youngest son, Rick, and married a man named Roger Caldwell. They were raising horses in Colorado. Aware that horses had been raised on the Congdon Estate in Duluth, I could see where that might make her happy.

Elisabeth Congdon

Velma Pietila

In 1977 the big news story on TV was that heiress, Elisabeth Congdon, and her personal nurse, Velma Pietila, had been found dead in the

Glensheen Mansion. The nurse had been bludgeoned to death with a brass candlestick and Elisabeth, adored by all who knew her and paralyzed by a recent stroke, had been smothered with a satin pillow. I couldn't believe it! How could this have happened? Elisabeth Congdon had lots of security; cooks on the premise, gardeners in their own building, and a nurse at her side. I became absorbed in the case, reading every article I could find and listening to every snippet of information. The Duluth community and police all over Minnesota were working on this crime. Within a few days the police were talking about the chance this was an inside job designed by her daughter, Marjorie—my Mrs. LeRoy—who was in need of money. "Never!" my inner voice screamed. The Marjorie I knew was gentle, kind, loving, and intelligent and would never do anything like this to her own mother. I couldn't accept that this woman was capable of such horror. I was sure she would be vindicated soon. But the news got worse over time.

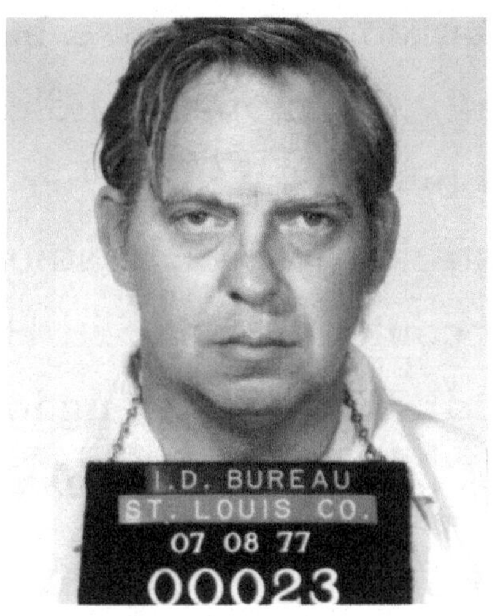

Roger Caldwell

Marjorie's second husband, Roger Caldwell, was indicted and imprisoned for murder. He claimed until his dying day he hadn't killed anyone and was released years later for lack of proof. During the hearing, it was stated that the murders were all about money. My inner voice started wondering if Marjorie had been involved to some extent, perhaps giving security information to her husband? I had heard that Richard LeRoy divorced Marjorie because she couldn't control her spending. The new little voice inside me questioned whether she really could have afforded my lavish bridal shower? When she was found "not guilty" I put this all aside, wanting to believe she was the woman I had adored years ago. That woman could not be capable of such evil.

Some years later, working at Miracle Mile Shopping Center in St. Louis Park, I had business with the daughter of Richard Hagen, owner of the Hagen Electric Company. She was telling me how upset her family was with their father's new bride. She said he had married Marjorie Congdon Caldwell in 1981. The newlyweds had known each other in Minnesota when they were both young and now resided in Arizona. This woman's family believed Marjorie was bilking their father out of large sums of money. I was shocked and told her that I'd known Marjorie when she was a young mother and admired her. The Hagen daughter became angry with my defense of Marjorie and shouted that her family was trying to legally put a stop to the drain of money and loss of the family business. My heart was hurting again; voices were talking from inside me.

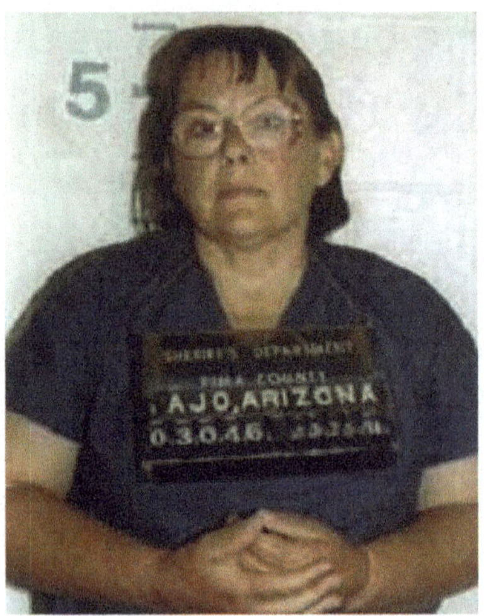

Marjorie Congdon

A few years later, an article in the local newspaper announced that Richard Hagen had died in his house in Arizona and the police suspected he had been poisoned. I learned that Marjorie Congdon LeRoy Caldwell Hagen had been arrested, found guilty, and sent to prison for his murder. Later, I was told she had needed money badly and was burning down homes and garages to collect the insurance money. Subsequently, I learned Marjorie was involved with the poisoning. How could I have been so wrong about this special lady in my past? I had been making excuses to myself that this woman could not have done such evil things. Not while she was in her right mind, so I rationalized that she must have developed some virulent form of mental illness.

White Lace Peignoir

By 1980 everything in me was questioning, my heart picking at my soul. Had I unconsciously accepted Marjorie's power and pristine appearance as the most acceptable way to live because my special woman had made me feel so important and rich? At home alone I thought about the lace peignoir from my honeymoon. It was wrapped in white tissue paper, still in its glistening gold box. Although it was luxurious and beautifully sexy, it was not comfortable to wear and over time I had not put it on. It represented hundreds of dollars wasted on a luxury that went against the grain of my upbringing.

Youth, the young girl years, is such an impressionable time! I believe my young brain had soaked up the lavish environment with no thought of guilt or consequences. My soul asked, had Marjorie spent money she really couldn't afford in order to give me the gift? I would never know for sure.

I removed the lace peignoir from the tissue, held it up to my face, and sighed, feeling so confused. With mixed feelings, I walked out to our burning barrel in the backyard, threw it in, and lit the match. Quickly, up in flames it went; white covered metal buttons, white translucent pear pearls, lace upon lace with satin ribbons, all up in flames in a minute. As I watched it burn I wondered why

I could not have seen the flaws in a woman who had proven to be truly mad and evil? Later, words written by a close friend to Marjorie summed it up: "She lied and lied and believed the things she lied about. She was charming and illogical all at the same time."

Deja Vu

Like a bad penny, gone but always found again, this story with truths in the innocence and naivety of a young woman came back to me when my son, Doug, called. "Your granddaughter is planning to have her destination wedding on the balcony of the Congdon Mansion in Duluth."

"What!" I exclaimed. I was aware that both she and her fiancée had graduated from the University of Minnesota in Duluth two years earlier. I knew they both worked in retail stores in Duluth and were dedicated to the UMD community. I thought, how could one piece of Real Estate run in and out of my life like a string of pearls vs. rocks, leaving my mind with scenes of nature's natural beauty, wealth, and evil. In an ironic twist of fate, both my wedding and my granddaughter's some fifty years later would be tied to the same woman. Was my past coming back to haunt me?

This macabre mansion looked to my eyes like the house of the extremely rich that had become Duluth's tourist attraction and had earned people's fascination with its horrors. My favored song giving me lasting memories was written by Dan Seals, sung by Crystal Gail, called "Everything that Glitters is not Gold." What sadness that this architectural, glorious piece of Real Estate which had been the Congdon's home for decades and had a large role in the growth of Duluth and history brings sadness to my mind.

A tour of the mansion years before had resulted in a dark feeling of foreboding that I still carry with me. On that tour I had encountered dark velvet drapes; classic oak-carved antique furniture upholstered in velvet; crystal chandeliers; carved oak paneling on the walls and staircases; fireplace after fireplace of porcelain and marble; and Italian and porcelain tiles everywhere, even in the bedrooms, kitchen, and bathrooms. There was luxury beyond my imagination—but no sunlight. That, along with its huge size, had produced a dark, damp feeling of loneliness within my soul. The spirit of the house felt cold and ghostly.

I asked my granddaughter to consider another location for her wedding, one without such a horrid history. Through research over the years I had learned that several workers had fallen to their death while hoisting the expensive interior designed walls, staircases, and ceramic tiles imported from Europe up the huge, slick rock walls to the Congdon estate. I could not deny those deaths and the deaths of two helpless women at the hand of a woman who, as a child, may have, at some level, been affected by the trauma of this huge haunted house. The whole scenario bothered me and I did not want my granddaughter to start her married life in such a depressing location. But, I had to concede, it was their decision, as well it should be.

Despite my misgivings, I received a beautiful invitation to the wedding and reception. It was to be held in the lower dining room area of the Congdon Mansion. My granddaughter knew I wouldn't miss her wedding for anything, especially not haunts from many years past.

There was much excitement in our family. Mother and daughter, both creative artists, made all of the decorations for the reception; twinkling white lights strung around the mostly underground windows, and copper, silver, and gold metal trims on each table with individual small copper half-circle cement balls hollowed out and filled with eye-catching green succulent cacti gracing the centers. Shades of white and green flowers decorated the head table.

The wedding service was held on the outdoor balcony overlooking the luxurious garden and pond where many guests were seated. After the service each of the guests was offered a guided tour of the mansion. Despite the festivity, I was uncomfortable in the house and couldn't dispel the feeling of gloom. I chose not to join the group; instead, I sat in the reception area until my family returned from the tour. As I waited in that underground area, everything felt damp from moisture in the ceiling and walls, compliments of Lake Superior. I am allergic to mold and could sense it, enhancing my mood of gloom and doom. Maybe it was because I was dwelling on the horrible knowledge of the lower window, broken so that a killer, presumably Roger Caldwell, could gain access to kill the two women. All of it was overwhelming me.

The food served by the catering service was superb. The love between the bride and groom was obvious; seeing them so happy made me feel good. My daughter and youngest granddaughter stayed close to me the entire evening, which helped me feel at peace with this special event. Sitting quietly, thinking, I could not help but know I would never want to live in this enormous house—I would lose my mind in the darkness—but to the reality of my human self, the luxury was still impressive. Despite my misgivings about the past, a small part of it is still with me, embedded in my love of antique furniture, crystal glass of all kinds, and Tudor style architecture that is now reflected in my home and its furnishings.

Even though memories of Marjorie Congdon and the Glensheen mansion trigger feelings of remorse that I, as a young, impressionable girl so many years ago, could have been taken in by the trappings of such luxury, I love and respect Lake Superior, where it all began, and regard it as Minnesota's ocean.

I ♥ duluth

Duluth Glensheen Mansion

Solid oak doors opened

A tall man in black appeared

Bowed slightly bending on his cane

Said, "Good afternoon" and that his name was

James

He ushered me toward Reception

Where under a solid gold ceiling

    A carved white alabaster lantern hung.

About to take a seat

A voice called out, "Please follow me."

She led me past the Smoking Room

Which did not accommodate my sex,

And further down the hallway

Until we reached our destination

"Please step inside," she said.

"I'd offer you a seat, but these chairs are very old

    They've already served their time.

"The walls are of mahogany
The fireplace built of red marble from Algiers."
Then she quickly turned and led me out.
She stopped inside a room nearby
Where walls were lined with books
And easy chairs in a window nook
Beckoned me to sit and look
    Out upon the giant lake
    And watch the ships pass by
"No time for that," she quickly said
    And hurried out,
And up the grand staircase carved of oak,
Where on the landing sunshine streamed
Through a stained glass window.

She led me in and out of bedrooms
Each with their private bath
And tiled and marbled fireplaces
To warm them from the cold winter winds
Which howled across the Great Lake
That lay just beyond the gauzy curtained windows.

Burke

We came upon a suite of rooms
At the far end above the kitchen
"Servants Quarters," she announced.
A peak in one showed a Singer Machine
On top an old worktable, instead of
Perfume bottles atop a dressing table.

We hurried down the backstairs just wide enough
for one
      Where once-upon the servants trod
And came into the kitchen
A glass cupboard held some books
      To show them how to cook.

Led through the pantry I stood in awe
On the edge of a Breakfast Room
      Encased in square green tiles
      And potted ferns to guard the window
"Most expensive room of the house," she remarked,
"For each tile cost five to seven dollars apiece,
And that's the price when the house was built."

STORMS in the Northland

No time to linger—the hour was getting late
We progressed to the formal dining room
Where a table to seat more than twenty
        Held center stage
And underneath, a Persian rug
Richly hued in reds and blues
Waited to catch discarded crumbs

Down more stairs we sped until
We reached the bowels of the house
The Play Rooms for the wealthy and
The Work Rooms for the servants.

The clock struck the hour—it was now time to depart
I did not want
        To overstay my welcome
I did not want
        To find a wood carved pineapple lying on the guest bed
That would be too embarrassing,
        So I swiftly drifted thru the basement door.

Author—Mary Henderson (Revised 2020)

Learn More

Over the years, I have found much information on the Glensheen Mansion, the Glensheen Estate, and the owners, Chester and Claire Congdon. Their gifts to Duluth are remarkable—both money and land, including Congdon Park in Duluth.

In 1998 Sharon Hendry researched and published the book *Glensheen's Daughter*.

In 2002 *Secrets of the Congdon Mansion* was written by Joe Kimball, a Star Tribune reporter who had followed the story for 30 years. Marjorie Congdon LeRoy Caldwell Hagen was sent to prison for involvement in the death of Richard Hagen and for setting fires in homes and garages for the insurance money. She was also found to be involved in the death of Roger Sammis in Arizona. She was released from prison in 2009.

In 2003 *Will to Murder* was published by Gail Feichtinger. The book was written with the help of John DeSanto and Gary Waller, the detectives who processed the scene of the murder and caught Roger Caldwell. The book tells of Marjorie's obsessions for acquiring things, tiring of them quickly, and often never even removing the tags from her very expensive, never used purchases. The book describes how Marjorie even attempted to kill her horse when it grew older, and her fondness for setting fires.

In 2013 a book was published by Suzanne Congdon LeRoy, *Nightingale: A Memoir of Murder, Madness, and the Messenger of Spring,* praising and honoring the memory of her beloved grandmother, Elisabeth Congdon, and the Congdon family's involvement in nursing and the Red Cross, as well as memories of her grandmother's personal nurse, Velma Pietila.

A book written for tourists and travelers, *Over Minnesota,* by Jim Klobuchar and Jerry Stebbins, illustrates the natural beauty of Minnesota and includes magnificent pictures of the Glensheen Manor on Lake Superior.

Gordon was instrumental in my love of Lake Superior and Grand Marais. He spent many years vacationing in a RV in that town. Both are considered our Large Lakes as if we had an ocean front.

Part 2

Two Old Lady's Adventures

y dreams of adventures around the United States were finally coming true. My husband and I invested in a used Winnebago Spirit. It was striking, with bright stripes and letters in jade and burgundy on the side. It was small, so I could easily drive and park it, and it was air conditioned. Wow; traveling in luxury, wherever we wished to go. We had our own bed (I always worried about bedbugs in motels), we could take our much-loved dogs, and we had a private bathroom right at our fingertips. Road trips were my idea of heaven; however, my husband's idea of heaven was his recliner at home. So, I often asked friends if they would like to take a road trip with me to Northern Minnesota.

My neighbor and friend, Hannah, said she would like to, and I was thrilled. Northern Minnesota had been my favorite stomping ground for years. Hannah had endured two hip replacements, infection, and then rehab, and while she walked with a cane, she was finally feeling well. She was ready to get out of the house and felt she deserved an adventure as a reward. Climbing the RV steps with a cane could be challenging, though, and her medical needs were serious. She was still a bit weak and fragile. Still, Hannah and I had fun over the years.

She had an adventurous personality and was always willing to try new things. She was eccentric (neighbors told me she was weird). She loved going out to eat at restaurants, as did I, but her idea of cooking was cold cereal and beans eaten right out of the can. I worried this would not help get her strength back.

Her husband had passed away many years before. Most of Hannah's time was spent alone, albeit with her pet Korean pig who lived in a huge dog kennel in her kitchen. He was gray and white with some pink skin, sparse pieces of hair sticking out here and there, and about as big as a cocker spaniel. He listened to her every word and really liked to eat—a lot—and what goes in comes out. He would run around and around in her fenced yard and then come back into the house. He was well trained, like a family dog. She adored him.

Hannah loved dogs, horses, and rodeos. Her daughter was involved with horses, but they did not get along. Hannah was not a cook or housekeeper. She had a quirky personality that I found interesting. She seemed unhappy, but I suspected she mostly felt alone.

"Do you think you are strong enough to get in and out of the RV with your cane?" I asked.

She said, "I really need to try something to gain confidence and strength, plus I could use a real vacation."

I said, "Let me see what I can plan." My decision was partly selfish; I wanted to know if I could manage a trip efficiently, taking care of the RV bathroom, driving, and parking the large vehicle.

When purchasing the RV, I researched travel sites and areas to see. I saved every advertisement, and one stood out: Camper's Paradise, on Lake Belle Taine in Nevis, Minnesota. It was 11 miles west of Walker, Minnesota. The description listed a 55-acre island with miles of sandy swimming beach. It sounded exciting and inviting for two elder women needing to rest and relax for a few days. Hannah agreed, and so in August 2015 we set out on our adventure up North. Hannah said, "I am so excited. Let's go!" I researched many places to see on the way.

Our first stop was Munsinger and Clemens Gardens near St. Cloud, Minnesota. The highly advertised gardens, tourists said, were beautifully manicured, balancing color and textures with native trees and plants. They featured all varieties of bushes, vines, and flowers, including giant oak, hemlock, and pine trees. There were hundreds of rose bushes, which are not easy to maintain in Minnesota's unpredictable weather. Roses are one of my favorite flowers. There were unique, cape-cod-like buildings, arches covered in flowers, walking paths, and fragrance that made this an inspiring adventure.

Hannah raved about the gardens, walked without great effort, and was ecstatic about the visit. The landscape of these spectacular gardens was designed well for people using canes or strollers, allowing them to see each different flower and bush.

Hannah and I slowly walked until exhaustion pushed us back to the RV. We were off to our destination for the night. We discussed the wonderful experience at the gardens, the great smells of the different flowers, and the many, many colors of blooms, as well as the adventure we would have going forward. The Campers Paradise ad called their location "Goat Island."

We drove hours north, watching nature's beauty of rustic pine trees at every turn, farm after farm, and horses, cows, and chickens along the way. We saw many swamps and small lakes, a must for Minnesota's Land of 10,000 Lakes. The most peaceful, natural hills and valleys kept us astounded. From log houses, mobile homes, and boat houses, to stacks of split wood, to huge ranches, we enjoyed it all. We made many potty stops, snacked along the way, and chatted. Hannah was patient, a good navigator, and kept smiling even on the back roads.

We had a bit of confusion on highway #34. Many strings of islands are near "Goat Island." When we arrived at our site at 4:00 P.M. on Wednesday afternoon, I was queasy. The entry into the resort island was an extremely narrow pathway: only gravel, rock, and sand, a single lane, with the lake on both sides and a very long road into the resort. A Volkswagen bug would be hard pressed not to have one tire in the water on all sides. The sand was soft and I knew one jerk of the hand could trip our large house on wheels into the lake. *Where is my courage?* I asked myself. *Try!*

We moved forward ever so slowly, with white knuckles and one side of the tires sloping into water and sand. Finally, I made it into the office area and met the receptionist. Hannah was anxious. I was shocked that we were in heavy woods, likely filled with bears and large animals. Fear was overtaking me; my gut was telling me I had made a wrong decision. We were two elder ladies, both with issues walking, and there was no even ground anywhere in sight.

The receptionist gave us our lot number and a map to find it. As I proceeded, I noticed the extremely dark forest, broken trees and bushes everywhere, but no sandy beaches. When we arrived at the marked lot, I really started to tremble. There was no flat ground, no overhead lighting, and no lighting hookup.

As we stepped out of the RV, we were walking on multiple rocks, piled sticks, debris, brush, holes in the dirt, and downed trees. The final scare was a sign that read, "Beware of Bears and Critters." These two old ladies did not know what was needed for a heavily wooded campsite, on the edge of multiple conjoining rivers, in a parking spot with no lighting or electricity. It was not what I had pictured.

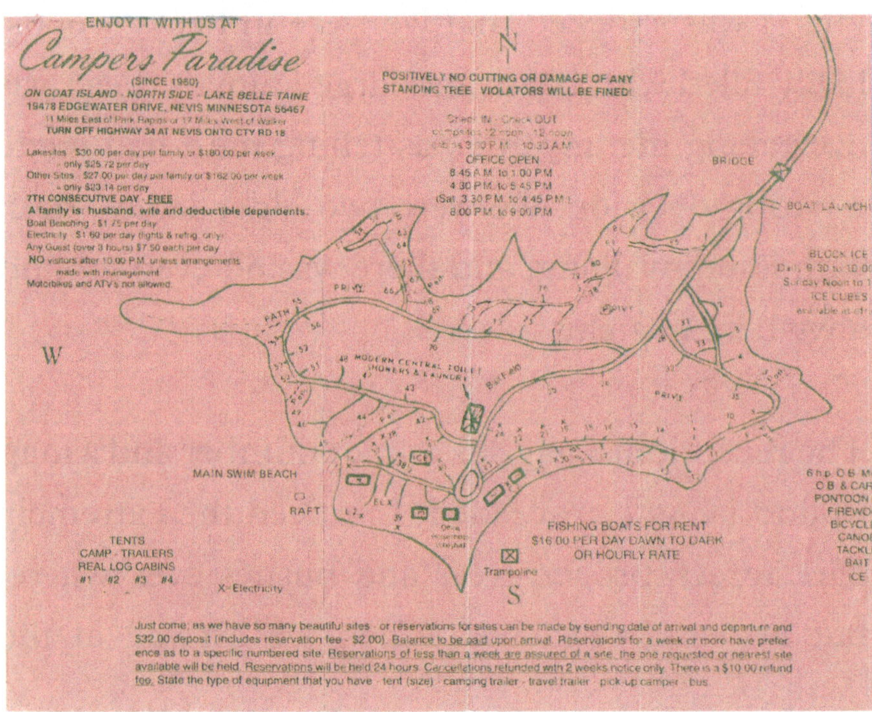

H. R. "CHRIS" and JEAN SWAGGERT

Camper's Paradise

ON GOAT ISLAND · NORTH SIDE · LAKE BELLE TAINE
19478 EDGEWATER DRIVE · NEVIS, MINNESOTA 56467

Dear Fellow Campers:

Have you been looking for a better place to go camping? We looked too and found a real "Campers' Paradise". We thought you would like to know about this wonderful campground. We are sure you will be as delighted with it as we are. This is a place for the true camper who appreciates natural beauty and privacy. This unique campground is on a 55 acre island that has a causeway and bridge from the mainland so you can drive to your campsite. Each site is approximately 100 feet apart in beautiful woods so that you can enjoy privacy.

Fishing is excellent all around the island as there are walleyes, northerns, crappies, sunfish, bass and muskies.

Lake Belle Taine where "Campers' Paradise" is located, is six miles long and about one mile wide and connects by river to many other lakes being the bottom lake of the famous Mantrap Chain.

Getting back to this fabulous campground, "Campers' Paradise", we have a central, modern restroom, shower and laundry building with plenty of hot water, a ball field, water trampoline, beach volleyball and horseshoe courts. There are swings and a slide for the small children, too. There are many species of birds and wildlife to see while biking and hiking around the island.

"Campers' Paradise" will be open Friday before Memorial Day to Labor Day. It is located approximately 200 miles northwest of Minneapolis/St. Paul and 100 miles east of Fargo, ND, 11 miles east of Park Rapids or 17 miles west of Walker via Hwy No. 34. At Nevis take County Road 18 on the north side of Lake Belle Taine 3 miles west following our signs, or thru Dorset - take County Road 18 east. There is no restriction as to the number of days you may spend with us. Also pets are welcome but must be on a leash, kept quiet and cleaned up after. For your convenience there are churches, doctors, a hospital, shopping, theaters, restaurants, horseback riding, golf (one of the finest public golf courses we have ever played), and the Mississippi River Headwaters nearby. The 27 mile Heartland, paved, bicycle trail from Park Rapids to Walker is only 1-1/2 miles from Campers' Paradise.

There are three rustic, real log cabins with large screen porches, that rent for $310.00 per week. Each cabin has two double beds, bedding, dishes, refrigerator, stove with oven and a boat. An extra double bed is $68.75 per week, a single bed is $48.50 per week. Please send a $160.00 deposit with your reservation.

Be sure to tell all your friends about it! We'll be glad to hear from you for any information or suggestions. Please send the name and address of anyone who would be interested and we will send them a letter, too.

Your enthusiastic camper friends since 1960,

H. R. "Chris" & Jean Swaggert

Campers' Paradise
19478 Edgewater Drive, Nevis, Minnesota 56467
Open Memorial Day weekend to Labor Day
NO PHONE - PLEASE WRITE

Winter Address
September 15 to May 15
19604 State 34
Park Rapids, Minnesota 56470

Campers' Paradise

The necessities—at bare minimum—were proper hiking boots and two trekking poles, NOT our light tennis shoes and shorts without mosquito spray. The ad—upon reading again later—said, "electricity $1.60 per day," but my mind read *many RV hook up sites*. My mind read *natural beauty* as trees and bushes, not fallen trees and brush everywhere. I read Walker and remembered tourist attractions and a fun learning experience. If I had been an experienced (smart) camper, I would have thought of heavy boots, bug spray, and the high probability of bears. Of course, I didn't know to take wood pieces for the fire pit (not even matches); I only remembered the statement, "You cannot take fire wood into a new campsite due to infestations of bugs."

As dark approached around 5:00 P.M., I said, "Hannah, this is not a good idea; I am sorry."

She quickly agreed and said, "Let's get out of here."

As I drove out, I told the receptionist I made a mistake; this site was too rustic for two old ladies and we were not staying. We rushed to get back on the narrow strip of land and sand to get us back to the mainland. It was nearing dusk, and I was having visions of the wheels sinking into the water. When we arrived on the mainland, I took a deep breath. Hannah, now very tired, said, "What should we do?"

After taking a moment to settle my nerves, I remembered a lovely RV park right across highway #18 on the edge of Lake Mille Lacs. It was Wednesday, so they may not have every site reserved. First, we needed to eat supper. I was very tired from driving, and I knew Hannah would love the large buffet at Grand Casino in Garrison, Minnesota. They serve a variety of foods and have kind people serving, shiny flat floors for walking, and soft padded chairs.

As we headed to Garrison and faced two more hours of driving, we stopped at the campground to make sure we had a place to stay after supper.

I smiled and quit worrying when the manager said, "Yes, we have a spot; yes, we have an electric hookup there; yes, it has a flat patio style area."

I said, "Yes, here is my money. Thank you!" The lot was small even for my small RV and right near the ditch, but it was the most gorgeous view of the lake (Minnesota's "ocean view"). There was a cement area under the rig and lush green grass all over. We set up our camp chairs, each with an attached table for drinks and food, and prepared the coffee pot to automatically make coffee in the morning. It was a perfect spot to relax, sit back, watch the water roll, and visit the next morning.

Ready for camping, we left for the casino buffet. So many options of good fish, beef, pork, and chicken prepared to perfection, plus many desserts, for $10.00. We both could relax. After all day driving, Hannah riding, every muscle was ready for sleep. We enjoyed a short conversation about what happened and discussed what we would go to see tomorrow. It was warm and clear, with stars shining over the lake. Hannah was comfortable in bed, so I didn't think to turn on the NOAA radio for news. When traveling I rarely turn on the radio, though I do carry an emergency cell phone and feel safe.

The RV beds were so comfortable with a four-inch-thick medical pad on each bed. There were beige fabric louvers covering the windows, and we could slide the side window above our bed open for fresh lake air. There is a standard-size bed right next to the bathroom that I thought was best for Hannah should she need it during the night. The table near the kitchen turned into a twin bed.

When I got into bed, I noticed the wind over the lake was blowing harder than when we got back from dinner, but I was so tired I just rolled over and started to sleep. Within hours, Hannah and I awoke to rain pounding the top and sides of the rig. Moments later, the rig started to shake; pounding rain and hail on metal made an echoing noise; and then the rig started rocking side to side. I was very frightened when I saw flames shooting out of the electric plug-in. Bang! The receptor blew up. Instantly the flames were gone, the plug was black, and we lost power. I knew the RV could roll over into the ditch, so I suggested that the safest place for Hannah was inside the tiny bathroom. She kindly asked if I could squeeze in also.

I said, "If I am going to die, I prefer it be in my bed with foam mattress, pillows, and blankets wrapped around me." The rig rolled from side to side. I was sure it was going to roll on its side, but it didn't. I thanked God and Winnebago for the strong RV that did not tip over in the high winds. The noise and movement were extremely frightening. After what seemed like forever, the noise was gone. Hannah shouted she was safe and back in bed. I knew morning would bring lots of damage around us but for now we needed to get some sleep.

At sunrise I opened the door. The coffee and lounge chairs we had set up were gone. The horror of the grounds brought tears. There was damage, trees broken off just above ground level and some near or on other camper's rigs and tents. There was debris, chairs, and fishing gear in the ditch, including our chairs and table. The main office was not crushed but had damage, and there were police cars and trucks everywhere. I inspected the RV (Spirit) and found burn marks from when the plug connecter was hit. There were leaves and twigs everywhere but no real damage to the body or tires, nothing I felt would stop us from driving home, and I was sure the electric cords could be fixed. Hannah was so nervous, shaking and asking me please take her home. With the city responding to help others, we felt it best to pick up our chairs and items near the RV. We realized how close to the large lake we were parked and were thankful we could just pick up things and head home.

Winds from the Aug. 9 storm are responsible for overturning and ravaging this boat dock on the northwest side of Mille Lacs Lake.

Morning storm whips Mille Lacs

by Vivian Clark
Messenger Staff Writer

Many area residents awoke early to the sound of thunder Tuesday, Aug. 9, as severe thunderstorms rumbled through the Mille Lacs Lake area. If the thunder didn't wake people up, the continuous buzzing of chainsaws beginning at daybreak probably did as the clean up began.

At approximately 4:26 a.m. the National Weather Service issued a severe thunderstorm warning affecting counties ranging from Aitkin to Wadena in central Minnesota. Andrew Tingler of the weather service said Doppler radar indicated storms produced quarter sized hail and destructive winds in excess of 78 mph.

"The storms organized early that morning. Thunderstorms take the winds

Storm damage to 22

PHOTOS BY BOB STATZ

...er in estimated 80-mph winds ...early morning on Aug. 9.

ls for billing changes

$9,000 to $10,000 per year by raising the rate per 1,000 gallons by 25 cents for water and sewer.

Among the roughly 200 Onamia...

As far as the rate hike goes, Council Member Mark Loch pointed out that Onamia's sewer rates will still be much...

The area residents and our campground compan-
ions were awakened in the night, as we were, to
sounds of thunder, rain, hail, and wind. On Tuesday, August 9th, 2015, a severe thunderstorm
rumbled through the Mille Lacs Lake area. As we
awoke, we knew there was damage by the buzzing of chainsaws beginning at daybreak. Then the
announcement at 4:26 A.M.: the National Weather

Service issued warning of severe storms that affected counties ranging from Aitkin to Wadena in Minnesota. The Doppler radar indicated storms producing quarter-sized hail and destructive winds of 78mph to 84mph to ground surface, which bent trees all along the left side of Lake Mille Lacs.

At the time we thought it was a tornado, but we were told it was called straight line winds. They caused so much damage, it was unbelievable. There were so many power outages including everyone in the RV lot. Everywhere we looked there were trees down to the ground, downed electric wires, and broken power poles. The entire city of Garrison was hit the hardest, with extensive damage in an area 25 miles wide and 40 miles long. The high winds took out docks and flattened trees along the ditches. The Mille Lacs Energy Cooperative had power outages to 3500 customers. Later I learned that electric crews worked 16 hours a day to restore power.

As we left the campground, my neighbor and friend was so upset and anxious to be back in her home.

When we arrived at her home, Hannah said, "I am so thankful for my lovely large home and lawn." Then added, "Please do not ever take me on one of your adventures again." My friend and neighbor's life came to an end on January 5, 2020 after years of health issues.

Rivershore Books

www.rivershorebooks.com

info@rivershorebooks.com

Made in the USA
Coppell, TX
18 August 2023

20415361R20044